MW00680362

# *(Un)remarkable*

## TEN ORDINARY WOMEN
## WHO IMPACTED THEIR WORLD
## FOR CHRIST

*foreword by*
**NANCY DEMOSS WOLGEMUTH**

© 2022 *Revive Our Hearts*
First printing, 2022

Published by *Revive Our Hearts*
P.O. Box 2000, Niles, MI 49120

ISBN: 978-1-934718-87-2

Printed in the United States of America.

All rights reserved. No part of this publication may be reproduced in any form without permission from the publisher, except in the case of brief quotations embodied in other works or reviews.

Edited by Anne Buchanan, Micayla Brickner, Erin Davis, Laura Elliott, Katie Laitkep, Hayley Mullins, and Mindi Stearns.

Cover design by Lauren Davis. Typography and interior design by Austin Collins.

Scripture quotations are from the ESV® Bible (The Holy Bible, English Standard Version®), Copyright © 2001 by Crossway, a publishing ministry of Good News Publishers. Used by permission. All rights reserved.

# Contents

# *Foreword*

If you took a moment and opened your Bible to the "great hall of faith" found in Hebrews 11, you'd find a list of familiar names: Noah, Abraham, Sarah, Moses, Rahab, David . . . Have you ever considered why the Holy Spirit inspired the writer of Hebrews to preserve these names for us? Why God sees fit to pass on the stories of *so many* individuals through His Word?

The bookshelves in my home are lined with biographies. Since I was a child, I have treasured the stories of faithful saints like George Müller, Hudson Taylor, Gladys Aylward, and many more (including many of the women highlighted in this resource). **I am passionate about encouraging the Church to pass these stories on from one generation to the next.**

Though many of my favorite biographies contain stories of men and women God used to do extraordinary things, most of the subjects were ordinary people—you might even call them unremarkable. Some of them had great limitations and significant obstacles to overcome. But these people trusted in an extraordinary God and He used them in extraordinary ways. On the pages of my Christian biographies, I've discovered time and time again that in God's kingdom the true greats are humble people whose lives declare, "It's not about me; it's about Jesus."

Hebrews 11 gives snapshots of many of the heroes of our faith, whose lives should challenge us. But turn the page to Hebrews 12, and your focus will shift away from stories of individuals and toward the One who writes every story.

> Therefore, since we are surrounded by so great a cloud of witnesses, let us also lay aside every weight, and sin which clings so closely, and let us run with endurance the race that is set before us, looking to Jesus, the founder and perfecter of our faith, who for the joy that was set before him endured the cross, despising the shame, and is seated at the right hand of the throne of God. (Heb. 12:1–2)

I hope you will keep this firmly in mind as you read about the women profiled in this booklet. Study how they ran their race. Admire how they exercised faith in God and were emboldened to lay aside every weight, every distraction, every hindrance, and the sins that tend to cling to us all. Cheer for those who endured the race God set before them with exceptional joy and perseverance. But don't stop there. **May the stories of these women remind you that Jesus is the ultimate hero. He's the one worthy of celebrating. He's the one who is worthy of your attention and adoration as you run your own race of faith.**

At the end of your life, as loved ones gather to celebrate your story, may they add your name and mine to the list of (un)remarkable women who lived lives committed to the glory of our remarkable God.

Nancy DeMoss Wolgemuth
Founder, lead teacher of *Revive Our Hearts*

# Introduction

## Let Heroes of the Faith Teach You Today

### Colleen Chao

This morning I woke up in a warm bed with a roof over my head. I took a hot shower, brewed a pot of coffee, and enjoyed breakfast made from my well-stocked fridge and pantry. Electricity, phone, and plumbing worked at my beck and call.

These comforts and conveniences are both a gift and grief. They're a gift because God appoints us to our particular place in history, geography, and culture (Acts 17:26–27). This very location and set of circumstances are from Him. But the gift quickly turns to grief when my passion for eternal realities is dampened by an all-needs-met existence. This physical wealth can numb my soul, and I'm daily at risk of living in spiritual poverty.

What good is it to have everything I need at my fingertips yet lose the very essence of who I'm created to be (Luke 9:25)? I was made to love and serve others for Christ—to joyfully spread God's fame in my little corner of the world and beyond.

### KINDLING FOR MY SOUL

Whenever I lose sight of this truth and fall into a sluggishness of soul—a craving for all things convenient, a reticence to do hard things—I like to revisit some "old friends," Christian men and women who have long since passed into glory but whose lives have indelibly shaped my own. Even as a young teenager, I was spellbound by their stories. Reading Christian biographies kindled a fire in my soul that would spark countless decisions and desires for years to come.

The men and women I read about were real people with real frailties and failings (sometimes embarrassingly so), but they lived in a way that displayed the surpassing greatness of Christ. Their faith was rugged and resilient, unashamedly rooted in the hope of the gospel. They considered their sufferings and sacrifices well worth the eternal rewards awaiting them and proved it by giving up all manner of comfort, success, even life itself. **They didn't expect life to be easy, fulfilling, or successful. They expected to lay down their lives for the sake of their God and His kingdom work.**

## A BIGGER VIEW

It's hard to conceive of such selflessness and self-denial in a culture that promotes the antithesis. We're conditioned to vehemently value *our* autonomy, *our* "rights," *our* health, *our* comforts, to live in the superficial and act as if this earth, this time, is our permanent home. For the sake of our souls, we need a bigger view, a historical perspective, and the company of those who have gone before us.

The study of Christian history has largely (and sadly) been relegated to theological seminaries and Bible colleges. Most of us rely wholly on modern advice and methodologies, neglecting a wealth of proven wisdom in what Hebrews 12 calls "so great a cloud of witnesses" (v. 1). If we were honest, many of us would admit that our culture, peers, and social media hold more sway on our life trajectory than does the influence of days gone by. And sadly that can apply to our *Christian* culture, peers, and social media as well.

Today there are thousands of blogging, book-writing Christians on the scene, and many of them have good things to say, biblical insights to share, wise counsel to impart. **But if our spiritual nourishment consists largely of blogs and books written by modern-day men and women who have lived a mere three, four, or five decades in affluent America, we risk spiritual malnutrition.** We may be glutted with writing about God's love, about our personal griefs and journeys to recovery, and about applying the gospel to our modern-day messes. We may hear plenty of buzzwords like *community*, *authenticity*, and *wholeness*. But when was the last time you read an author who wrote like this?

> *Nothing will seem too much to have done or suffered, when, in the end, we see Him and the marks of His wounds; nothing will ever seem enough. Even the weariness of deferred hope will be forgotten, in the joy that is not of earth.*[1] *(Amy Carmichael, 1867–1951)*

Or this?

> *I remember, when I have preached at different times in the country, and sometimes here, that my whole soul has agonized over men, every nerve of my body has been strained and I could have wept my very being out of my eyes and carried my whole frame away in a flood of tears, if I could but win souls.*[2] *(Charles Spurgeon, 1834–1892)*

## A LENS FOR LOOKING AT CHRIST

Not only does reading Christian biography put iron into our souls, it is also extremely *practical* for daily life—giving us a richer, broader perspective on relationships, education, career, marriage, parenting, spiritual disciplines, politics, and ministry. C. S. Lewis said it gives us eyes to see "the controversies of the moment in their proper perspective." Lewis argued passionately for the reading of old books: "My own eyes are not enough for me, I will see through those of others. Like the night sky in the Greek poem, I see with a myriad of eyes, but it is still I who see."[3]

**These "others" Lewis referred to—the flawed but faithful believers from the past—are not meant to be the object of our gaze but rather to serve as a lens through which we see Christ more clearly.** As we look through their eyes, our own are lifted beyond our present circumstances, and we are strengthened to run our course well.

God has gifted us with a cloud of witnesses because our own eyes are not enough. Don't let the testimony of these lives be lost on you. Walk with them awhile, learn from their mistakes, consider their counsel, and imitate their love and obedience to God.

Colleen Chao writes about God's goodness in her life journey, which has included singleness, anxiety and depression, chronic illness, and stage-four cancer. Colleen makes her home near Boise, Idaho, with her husband, Eddie, their son Jeremy, "the cat," and Willow the dog. The woman in Christian history Colleen most admires is Amy Carmichael—for the way she loved Jesus and cared for others out of her many sufferings.

# Take It Home, Make It Personal

1. Describe the spiritual content you consume most regularly. Based on Colleen's definition, would you diagnose yourself with spiritual malnutrition?

2. Name some of the spiritual heroes who have shaped your faith. What aspects of their lives have helped you grow in love and obedience to God?

3. Read Hebrews 11–12:2, thanking God for providing you with the proven wisdom of "so great a cloud of witnesses."

# Mary Slessor
## The Great Mother of Many

### Jani Ortlund and Hugh Duncan

# CHAPTER 1: MARY SLESSOR

L*ife was tough for Mary Slessor.* She was born in 1848 near Aberdeen, Scotland, where workers were needed to work in textile mills. Her family lived in poverty. To contribute, she began working in a factory at age eleven and as a teenager she worked twelve-hour days, often coming home to find her father drunk. Though she described herself as "wee and thin and not very strong," she bravely stood up to her father when her family needed protection. Her blue eyes blazed. Her red hair appeared to be a picture of her fiery will. It was the same kind of tenacity she would later put on display when fending off a leopard in Africa.

Still, Mary's work ethic and tough will were not enough to meet her deepest needs. As a teenager, she recognized her sin and she asked Jesus to forgive her and make her new. She was eager to share the hope she had found in Christ even though she didn't fit the stereotype of a church-going girl. (It was unusual in that day for girls to go barefoot and climb trees like Mary did.)

Her unconventional style still proved effective for building God's kingdom. A gang of teenage boys once cornered Mary and edged closer while one boy swung a lead weight on a string. Mary stood courageously even as the lead brushed her face. The leader of the band dropped the rope and the entire gang agreed to go to church with Mary that night.

## STANDING UP FOR THE VULNERABLE

Mary knew the people of Scotland needed the gospel, but many churches were already engaged in that work. She realized hardly any churches existed in parts of Africa, and she felt the Lord drawing her heart there. At age twenty-eight, Mary sailed for Calabar (located in present day Nigeria).

Mary worried that her departure might put too much strain on her invalid mother and sole surviving sister. So she sought her mother's blessing. Her mother's faith-filled reply freed Mary to follow her calling: "You are my child, given to me by God, and I have given you back to Him. When He needs you and where He sends you, there I would have you be."[1] Mary never saw her mother again on this side of heaven.

In her homeland, Mary had combined a love for people with a tough willingness to confront sin and stand up against injustice. She did the same in her new surroundings. Out of love for the Africans she desired to reach with the gospel, she learned the Efik language and embraced many social customs as she bravely stood against the unjust practices of slavery, cannibalism, and tribal warfare.

Mary's aim in going to Africa was to help the poor and oppressed—particularly the women, who were considered nothing more than property. She begged God for guidance and help, writing home that "my one great consolation and rest is prayer."

When village chiefs died, their wives and slaves were often killed as well. Mary intervened and worked to save their lives. Once when she observed a trial in which boiling oil was poured into the hands of an eleven-year-old boy, Mary got involved and took the liquid into her own hands. Into a culture of death, Mary brought a message of life. To people often governed by cruelty, she taught love and kindness. And always, always, she spoke of her Savior, who was the answer to every human need. She never kept track of her accomplishments. "It comes back to this. Christ sent me to preach the gospel, and He will look after the results."[2]

She deliberately gave up everything for her Master and accepted the consequences without murmur or complaint. "Everything no matter how seemingly secular or small is God's work for the moment and worthy of our very best endeavour."[3]

## MA AKAMBA, *THE GREAT MOTHER*

Mary never married, though not for lack of a suitor. The mission board asked Mary to break her engagement to a fellow missionary and she complied, reasoning, "We alter things for the good of our children, and God does the same for us."[4] But the loneliness and isolation she lived with were not easy.

Though she had no child of her own to hold, Mary loved all children. She came to be called *Ma Akamba*, the Great Mother, and her house was a continual refuge for little ones. She cared for all who were brought to her, sometimes passing them back to their parents, other times comforting them on their way to heaven and then burying them in the ever-extending cemetery plot behind her hut.

One local practice she fought against was the superstitious killing of all twins at birth, after which their mother would be sent off into the jungle, alone and in disgrace. Mary had a mother's heart and rescued all she could, often carrying them for miles on foot to obtain tins of milk to feed them.

In order to protect one of these children, she once chased a leopard with a burning stick. In every danger, she saw God continue to work. "Had I not felt my Saviour close beside me, I would have lost my reason,"[5] she later wrote.

Mary faced dangerous animals and warring people with courage, but it was disease that caused her the most peril. She suffered from malaria and twice returned to Scotland to recover from illness.

Mary's love of people and strong sense of justice earned the respect of Africans and British colonizers. After returning to Nigeria, she became a vice-consul, settling disputes between people and tribes. She continued moving deeper and deeper inland, sharing the gospel with those who hadn't heard the truth.

## MAKE MUSIC EVERYWHERE

Mary Slessor lived—*really lived*—until she died. At the time of her death she had served nearly forty years in Africa and maintained her enthusiasm, sympathy, and humor all the way to the end. One coworker wrote, "She seemed to grow more wonderful the older and frailer she became." She died in an African hospital after arriving there by canoe.

Mary Slessor's life was a model of unselfish, dedicated, unwearied devotion to Christ. She wrote to a friend, "Don't grow up a nervous old maid! Gird yourself for the battle outside somewhere, and keep your heart young. Give up your whole being to create music everywhere, in the light places and in the dark places, and your life will make melody."[6]

## About Jani

Jani Ortlund, the vice president of Renewal Ministries, loves connecting women with the Word of God. Serving Christ through writing, speaking, and discipling is her chief passion in life. Jani, who podcasts at herestoresmysoul.org, and Ray, the president of Renewal Ministries, have four married children and fifteen grandchildren. One of the women from Christian history whom Jani greatly admires is Amy Carmichael. Jani is grateful for Amy's wholehearted devotion to Christ and her cheerful defiance as she pressed on no matter the cost to serve His purposes for her in her generation.

## About Hugh

Hugh Duncan serves as director of audio and video for *Revive Our Hearts*. He's married to Renae and is dad to Nora and Muriel. While working on audio projects about Billy Graham and Bill and Vonette Bright, he was struck by the influence of one woman from church history. Henrietta Mears, director of education at First Presbyterian Church of Hollywood, was a huge encouragement to a generation of leaders whose influence is still being felt today.

# Take It Home, Make It Personal

1. Mary Slessor considered her Savior the answer to every human need. In what ways has Jesus been the answer to the needs in your life and the lives of those around you?

2. Mary said, "Everything no matter how seemingly secular or small is God's work for the moment and worthy of our very best endeavor." What "small" tasks in your life are worthy of your very best endeavor?

3. As she grew older, Mary's coworkers said she became more wonderful. What can you do today that will help you grow into a more gracious, more devoted older woman?

_____

_____

_____

_____

_____

*"We lived dangerously . . .*
*And were never bored."*

CHAPTER 2

# Sabina Wurmbrand
## Radical Faithfulness, Beautiful Forgiveness

Leanna Shepard

## CHAPTER 2: SABINA WURMBRAND

In 1913 Sabina Wurmbrand was born into an Orthodox Jewish home in Romania. As she matured into adulthood, she "outgrew" her strict Jewish upbringing and chose to live a wild, immoral life.

While visiting an uncle, Sabina met the tall, handsome Richard Wurmbrand and quickly fell in love. She impulsively moved to Bucharest to be near him, and the blissful couple married on October 23, 1936. She hadn't believed her soon-to-be-husband when he warned her that life with him would not be easy, but she quickly discovered his words to be true.

Shortly after their wedding Richard came down with tuberculosis. During his severe illness Richard began reading the New Testament and came to see Christianity in a new light. It was not the repulsive, Jew-hating cult he had believed it to be.

As Richard's physical health strengthened, so did his understanding of the gospel. But while God was softening Richard's heart, Sabina was becoming resentful and anxious about the change she saw in her husband. On the day Richard went to be baptized, Sabina determined she would kill herself. But God had other plans. As her husband surrendered himself to baptism, God did a cleansing work in Sabina's own heart. She saw herself for who she truly was—a sinner in need of grace—and experienced firsthand the mercy and forgiveness of a loving Savior.

### LIFE AS A PRISONER

In 1945 Communists seized power in Romania. Richard Wurmbrand had gained a reputation for ministering to his oppressed countrymen during World War II and boldly preaching the gospel. Because of this the Communists watched him closely, and in 1948 the Secret Police arrested him, leaving Sabina alone to care for their young son, Mihai.

For Sabina, Richard's sudden disappearance began fourteen years of searching, praying, waiting, and hoping. Two years after his arrest, Sabina also found herself imprisoned for her faith in a camp where she experienced horrific living conditions and was forced to do harsh manual labor. The camp was filled beyond capacity with thousands of women of all backgrounds—nuns and prostitutes, Romas and activists, nobles and thieves, all sharing bunks and refuse buckets.

Though her body was held captive, Sabina's soul was still free, and it was clear to prisoners and guards alike that Sabina had something they did not. Her inexplicable peace and ability to extend love and forgiveness to her captors and cellmates baffled them all.

Sabina used every opportunity to tell others about Christ, risking punishment and torture. Although not exempt from occasional bouts of discouragement and doubt, she managed to hold on to courage and hope despite what she suffered.

After three years at the camp, Sabina was released. Three years later, after eight-and-a-half years in prison, Richard also was released—only to be rearrested a few years later. During his years in prison, Richard endured brutal treatment, spending years in solitary confinement in an underground prison cell and later being tortured mercilessly.

On more than one occasion during these years, with little or no word of Richard's whereabouts, Sabina was tempted to give up on him altogether, to divorce him or consider him dead and move on with life, as many other prisoners' wives had done. Once she even received official notification that he was dead. But God protected Sabina's heart and her marriage. How grateful she was that she had not given up when, after many long years of silence, she received a postcard in his handwriting that began, "Time and distance quench a small love, but make a great love grow stronger."[1]

After Richard was released for the second and final time, having endured years of horrific treatment, he joined Sabina and their grown son in their work with the underground church.

In a variety of locations, the church met in secret. "We lived dangerously," Sabina would later write in her autobiography, "And were never bored." Every detail of their gatherings had to be well thought-out in advance: the place, the hour, the location, the password—everything. Even with those precautions, they were often caught by the secret police or betrayed by informers. Those attending knew it was possible they would never return home. The ministers preached every sermon as if it was their last because it well might have been.

As friends and neighbors were whisked away by the police, Sabina discovered she was harboring bitterness against the informers. It was hard for her to understand why people would turn against their brothers and sisters.

After lying awake one night thinking about it, Sabina's eyes rested on a portrait of Christ hanging on the cross. She was reminded of some of Christ's last words before His death: "Father, forgive them, for they know not what they do" (Luke 23:34). She recognized the anger in her heart, and something within her changed. "How they thirsted, the betrayers, for forgiveness! Which I would not give them. Which in my bitterness I withheld." She resolved to show them love and expect nothing in return.

## A VOICE FOR THE UNDERGROUND CHURCH

In December of 1965 two Jewish Christian missions paid a ten-thousand-dollar ransom to the Communist government, allowing the Wurmbrand family to escape Romania. They eventually made their way to the United States, but they did not forget the plight of their people. Out of concern for persecuted believers, the Wurmbrands began The Voice of the Martyrs, a ministry dedicated to serving the underground church in places where Christians were persecuted.

Most of Sabina Wurmbrand's life was marked with intense suffering. She traversed valleys of deep pain and sailed through rough waters of fear and sorrow. But today she is remembered and honored for her faithfulness to Jesus and the forgiveness she showed others. For even amidst the years of seemingly insurmountable hardship, her heart continually reflected the love and compassion of her Savior.

### About Leanna

Leanna Shepard loves Jesus, mountains, blueberries, and spending time with family and friends. An ideal day for her starts with a hot cup of tea and ends with a good book. She is grateful for the women throughout history (both ancient and recent) who have pointed her to Jesus, including Hagar, Corrie ten Boom, and Elyse Fitzpatrick.

# Take It Home, Make It Personal

1. Sabina's life changed when she saw herself for who she truly was. When did you first see yourself as a sinner in need of grace?

2. While Sabina was imprisoned, the peace and love she displayed baffled her captors. Have you ever experienced unexplainable peace in the midst of a difficult moment?

3. Read Luke 23:13–34. Summarize what this passage reveals about forgiveness.

_____

_____

_____

_____

_____

_____

_____

_____

_____

_____

_____

_____

_____

_____

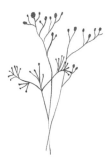

*"I give up myself, my life, my all,*
*utterly to Thee, to be Thine forever."*

# Betty Scott Stam
## A Life of Surrender

Nancy DeMoss Wolgemuth and Mindy Kroesche

## CHAPTER 3: BETTY SCOTT STAM

O ne of the challenges of complete surrender to Christ is that we don't know what lies ahead. Some of us might be more inclined to surrender if God would hand us a contract with all the details filled in. We want to see all the fine print so we can read it over, think about it, and then decide whether to sign on the dotted line.

But that's not God's way. God says instead, "Here's a blank piece of paper. I want you to sign your name on the bottom line, hand it back to Me, and let Me fill in the details. Why? Because I am God, because I have bought you, because I am trustworthy. You know how much I love you. So live for My glory and not your own independent, self-promoting pleasure."

### UNCONDITIONAL SURRENDER

Betty Scott Stam was a woman who trusted God to fill in the details. Born in 1906 in Albion, Michigan, she grew up in China, where her parents were missionaries. When she was seventeen years old, she returned to the United States for her last year of high school, then went on to college at Moody Bible Institute. During those years Betty penned a prayer that has become the petition of many other believers:

> Lord, I give up my own plans and purposes, all my own desires, hopes and ambitions, and I accept Thy will for my life. I give up myself, my life, my all, utterly to Thee, to be Thine forever. I hand over to Thy keeping all of my friendships; all the people whom I love are to take second place in my heart. Fill me now and seal me with Thy Spirit. Work out Thy whole will in my life at any cost, for to me to live is Christ. Amen.[1]

During Betty's years at Moody, God tested her commitment. Although Betty had always assumed that she, too, would serve as a missionary in China, the

Lord began drawing her attention to Africa, especially to the suffering of lepers. But could she lay down what she had thought was her calling, the place where her parents served and she had grown up, and give her life to service elsewhere?

During this time she was also drawn to a young man named John Stam, who planned to be a missionary in China. The tug on her heart must have been a powerful one. But clarity came when she decided to follow God wherever He led her. Through a poem she wrote and sent to her father, we can see her joy and peace at surrendering her desires and her future to the Lord.

> *I'm standing, Lord: There is a mist that blinds my sight.*
> *Steep, jagged rocks, front, left and right,*
> *Lower, dim, gigantic, in the night.*
> *Where is the way?*
>
> *I'm standing, Lord:*
> *The black rock hems me in behind,*
> *Above my head a moaning wind*
> *Chills and oppresses heart and mind.*
> *I am afraid!*
>
> *I'm standing, Lord:*
> *The rock is hard beneath my feet; I nearly slipped, Lord, on the sleet.*
> *So weary, Lord! and where a seat?*
> *Still must I stand?*
>
> *He answered me, and on His face*
> *A look ineffable of grace,*
> *Of perfect, understanding love,*
> *Which all my murmuring did remove.*
>
> *I'm standing, Lord:*
> *Since Thou hast spoken, Lord, I see*
> *Thou hast beset—these rocks are Thee!*
> *And since Thy love encloses me,*
> *I stand and sing.*[2]

God finally made the call to China clear. After completing her schooling, Betty returned there in 1931 to serve with the China Inland Mission (CIM). But the question of her relationship with John Stam still lingered. Although the two had expressed their feelings for each other, John still had one year of schooling to complete and had not yet been accepted into CIM. Choosing once more to leave her future in God's hands, Betty left for China with no formal commitment between them.

The following year John sailed for China to serve with CIM and was able to reunite with Betty. An engagement followed shortly. They married in October of 1933 and served together in the Anhui province. During the day they visited nearby villages to share the gospel; in the evenings they led meetings with another missionary in the area. The work was difficult, as the area was mountainous and the people extremely poor, but the Stams rejoiced at the opportunity God had given them to share the good news of Christ.

On September 11, 1934, their daughter, Helen Priscilla, was born. Three months later John, Betty, and their infant daughter were arrested by hostile Communist soldiers. After spending the night in a local prison, the soldiers forced them to march twelve miles to another town to be executed. They stopped for the night at the home of a wealthy man who had fled. Before they left the next morning, Betty hid her baby in the house inside a small sleeping bag. Then John and Betty were marched through the streets of the town, hands tightly bound and stripped of their outer garments.

A Christian shopkeeper tried to persuade the soldiers not to kill the couple. He, too, was dragged away to be killed. When John pleaded with the soldiers not to kill the man, the Communist leader ordered him to kneel, wielded a sword, and beheaded him. Still bound at her husband's side, Betty fell, no scream coming from her lips. Moments later the same sword ended her life.

Baby Helen was discovered thirty hours later by a local pastor. She was safe and warm, apparently none the worse for having gone all that time without nourishment. Inside her clothing the pastor found extra diapers and two five-dollar bills that Betty had pinned there—just enough to get the baby to safety.

## AT ANY COST

Betty was twenty-eight years old when she was killed. When she asked God as a college student to "work out Thy whole will in my life at any cost," she had no way of knowing what full surrender would cost her. Some might consider that cost too high. But Betty, having laid down her life for Christ, would not agree. She had relinquished all that she was and all that she had into Christ's hands for safekeeping.

A small group of believers found John and Betty's bodies and buried them on a hillside. Betty's gravestone read:

> Elisabeth Scott Stam, February 22, 1906
> "For to me to live is Christ, and to die is gain." Philippians 1:21
> December 8, 1934, Miaosheo, Anhui
> "Be thou faithful unto death, and I will give thee a crown of life."
> Revelation 2:10

God's plan for your life and mine will not look exactly like His plan for Betty Stam. But as followers of Christ, we, like Betty, are called to give up our own plans and embrace His will. As Betty herself said,

> When we consecrate ourselves to God, we think we are making a great sacrifice, and doing lots for Him, when really we are only letting go some little, bitsie trinkets we have been grabbing, and when our hands are empty, He fills them full of His treasures.[3]

## About Nancy

Nancy DeMoss Wolgemuth has touched the lives of millions of women through two nationally syndicated radio programs heard each day—*Revive Our Hearts* and *Seeking Him*. Her books have sold more than five million copies. Through her writing, podcasts, and events, Nancy is reaching the hearts of women around the world, calling them to freedom, fullness, and fruitfulness in Christ. Nancy is inspired by women like Selina Hastings, Countess of Huntingdon (1707–1791), who used her considerable resources and influence to help further the work of the first Great Awakening, foreign missions, and the care of infants and children who had been abandoned by their parents.

## About Mindy

*About Mindy*

Mindy Kroesche lives on a small acreage in the Midwest with her husband and two kids. She likes relaxing at the lake with her family, curling up with a cozy mystery, and finding out what coffee shops serve the best raspberry mochas. Mindy is inspired by the stories of women like Elisabeth Elliot, Gladys Aylward, and Corrie ten Boom who chose to trust and obey the Lord no matter what.

# Take It Home, Make It Personal

1. Can you think of a time when you, like Betty, had to surrender your own plans and purposes? Reflect on what you learned from that experience.

2. What phrase from Betty's poem stands out to you most? Why?

3. Read Psalm 116:15. Why do you think the death of saints is "precious" to the Lord?

# *Corrie ten Boom*
## Ordinary Woman, Extraordinary Faith

### Kelly Needham

## CHAPTER 4: CORRIE TEN BOOM

Great saints of previous generations can seem larger than life, gifted in unattainable ways, able to accomplish feats of great spiritual impact. But Corrie ten Boom, the youngest of four children, was not particularly outstanding. She had no unusual skills, no exceptional intelligence, no world-changing plans. Yet she emerges from the great cloud of witnesses to show us what God can do with extraordinary faith and radical obedience in the simplest of His people.

### A GREENHOUSE: HER EARLY YEARS

The household rhythm of Bible reading—morning and night—was as predictable in the ten Booms' home as the timing of the watches they fixed at their shop in the Dutch town of Haarlem. Corrie's parents, Casper and Cornelia, never considering their own lack and poverty, often gave away the last of what they had to help others. Corrie grew up in this greenhouse of Scripture study and sacrificial love.

Like most young women, Corrie hoped for a novel-worthy romance. But God clearly denied this dream when the love of her life introduced her to his fiancée. With her father's guidance, Corrie managed to surrender her dreams to God: "Lord, I give You the way I feel about Karel, my thoughts about our future—oh, You know! Everything! Give me Your way of seeing Karel instead. Help me to love him that way. That much."[1]

### RADICAL OBEDIENCE: WORKING IN THE UNDERGROUND

In 1942 Corrie, now fifty years old and still living with her older sister, Betsie, and their father in Haarlem, heard the first knock on their door from a fearful Jewish neighbor. The Nazis had occupied the Netherlands two years earlier. Jewish citizens were in danger. And the ten Booms could not ignore their Jewish friends any more than they could a hungry errand boy in the alley. Thus began their work with the underground movement to protect Jewish citizens.

As more timid knocks came, Corrie realized the danger of their home's location near police headquarters. So the family embarked on the complicated work of relocating Jews to houses in the country where they could hide without exciting the Germans' attention.

In all this work, **the ten Booms never desired to change the world but rather to obey the One who is truly in charge.** In Corrie's words,

> *My job was simply to follow His leading one step at a time, holding every decision up to Him in prayer. I knew I was not clever or subtle or sophisticated; if [our home] was becoming a meeting place for need and supply, it was through some strategy far higher than mine.*[2]

As the family's work continued, they housed Jews who were especially difficult to hide. As their very Jewish-looking resident Eusie told Corrie, "It seems to me that we're all here in your house because of some difficulty or other. We're the orphan children—the ones nobody else wanted."[3]

Fully aware it was only a matter of time before they were caught, the ten Booms continued to help. On February 28, 1944, the Nazis raided their home, and Corrie and her family were taken to prison. The ten Boom family, waiting on the floor of a gymnasium to be escorted to jail, ended that day the same way they had every day of their lives—with Bible reading and prayer. Corrie's father recited Psalm 119 from memory: "Thou art my hiding place and my shield: I hope in thy word. . . . Hold thou me up, and I shall be safe" (vv. 114, 117 KJV).

## GOD'S LOVE IS DEEPER: AT RAVENSBRÜCK

After three long months in prison (Corrie spending most of it in solitary confinement), Corrie and Betsie were transferred to a concentration camp in the Netherlands for another three months. It was only a foretaste of horrors to come.

On September 8, 1944, after a three-day "nightmare train ride" into the heart of Nazi Germany, the ten Boom sisters arrived at Ravensbrück concentration camp in Germany. But they still had hope because, by God's help, a Bible had miraculously made it with them, hidden in a pouch around Corrie's neck. Through yet another God-ordained moment, the precious package made it through the strip search and to the showers. "[When] we were herded into [the shower room], we were not poor, but rich. Rich in this new evidence of the care of Him who was God even of Ravensbrück."[4]

There at Ravensbrück—a place of naked examinations, beatings, lice and fleas, sickness and overflowing toilets, starvation and hard labor, freezing temperatures and threadbare blankets—God called Corrie and Betsie to be ministers of the gospel. All their years of ordinary, consistent, faith-filled obedience had prepared them to be ready and willing to bring His Word to hell itself.

> One thing became increasingly clear: the reason the two of us were here. From morning until lights-out, whenever we were not in ranks for roll call, our Bible was the center of an ever-widening circle of help and hope. Like waifs clustered around a blazing fire, we gathered about it, holding out our hearts to its warmth and light. The blacker the night around us grew, the brighter and truer and more beautiful burned the word of God.[5]

In the deepest pit imaginable, God's love was deeper still. In the darkest night, His Word shone all the brighter.

## LASTING FAITHFULNESS: HER LATER YEARS

Betsie died in Ravensbrück on December 16, 1944. Weeks later Corrie was released. Less than six months after that, Corrie opened a Christian rehabilitation center for war victims.

Barely a year after her release from Ravensbrück, Corrie published a book and began traveling to share her story. After one speaking engagement she faced a great test of faith: a former German guard and new believer approached her to shake her hand. He was one of the guards in front of whom she and Betsie had been forced to strip.

Aware of no strength within herself to extend her hand in forgiveness, she prayed. "Jesus, I cannot forgive him. Give me Your forgiveness."[6] The love God gave her in that moment helped her realize "that it is not on our forgiveness any more than on our own goodness that the world's healing hinges, but on His. When He tells us to love our enemies, He gives, along with the command, the love itself."[7]

Corrie spent her later years on a busier schedule than most half her age, traveling worldwide to share about God's deep love in dark places. Only a stroke in 1978 slowed her down. Those closest to her reported that she faced her final years and death with grace-filled endurance, fully surrendered to God's plan for her life and death.

Corrie ten Boom was an ordinary woman with profound hope in a faithful God. Though she didn't set out to change the world, her faith-filled, daily steps of obedience did just that.

## About Kelly

Kelly Needham hopes to convince as many people as possible that nothing compares to knowing Jesus. She teaches the Bible at her home church where she coleads a women's teaching program, training women to accurately handle the word of truth. She is the author of *Friendish: Reclaiming Real Friendship in a Culture of Confusion* and is a frequent blogger and speaker. Kelly and her husband, Jimmy, have four children and live in the Dallas, Texas, area. Corrie ten Boom is one of Kelly's favorite women in Christian history because she exemplifies the power of daily, ordinary obedience to God.

# Take It Home, Make It Personal

1. Corrie's family began their day with Bible reading and prayer even on the day they were waiting to be escorted to jail. What are your current Bible reading habits? How does the ten Booms' example impact the way you feel about the importance of Scripture?

2. Corrie said that when God "tells us to love our enemies, He gives, along with the command, the love itself." Is there someone you need to forgive today? Ask God to enable you to love that person as He has loved you.

3. Read Psalm 119:114, 117. How was God a hiding place for Corrie? How has God sustained you and kept you safe?

*"I should feel happy in the consideration of having left my native land, and my father's house, if by making this sacrifice, the kingdom of Christ would be promoted."*

CHAPTER 5

# Ann Hasseltine Judson
## A Deathward Life for Christ

Laura Elliott

## CHAPTER 5: ANN HASSELTINE JUDSON

How did a young girl go from being a New England socialite to a missionary pioneer, blazing a trail marked with devotion to Christ, love for her husband, and a passion for people? The way to her heart is through her words, as found in her letters and memoir.

### THOSE EARLY, HAPPY YEARS

Ann enjoyed a blissful childhood, coddled by her family in Bradford, Massachusetts, and given only the most basic of religious education. "I was early taught by my mother," Ann later wrote,

> *the importance of abstaining from the vices to which children are liable. . . . [so that] I should at death, escape that dreadful hell, the thought of which sometimes filled me with alarm and terror.*
>
> *I therefore made it a matter of conscience to avoid the above-mentioned sins, to say my prayers night and morning, and to abstain from my usual play on the Sabbath, not doubting that such a course of conduct would ensure my salvation.*[1]

Believing that "being good" secured her entrance to heaven and that she was able to achieve such goodness, Ann grew up happy and confident. And in her teen years, which were full of outings, balls, and parties, she abandoned the religious inclinations of her childhood. She reached a point when she was "rapidly verging toward eternal ruin. . . surrounded with associates, wild and volatile like myself." And yet she later remembered, she "often thought myself one of the happiest creatures on earth."

## CAPTURED BY LOVE

But God eventually took hold of young Ann Hasseltine's heart. After months of vacillating she found herself where stories of new life often begin:

> I felt myself to be a poor lost sinner, destitute of every thing to recommend myself to the divine favour . . . by nature, inclined to every evil way; and that it had been the mere sovereign, restraining mercy of God, not my own goodness, which had kept me from committing the most flagrant crimes. This view of myself humbled me in the dust, melted me into sorrow and contrition for my sins, induced me to lay my soul at the feet of Christ, and plead his merits alone, as the ground of my acceptance.[2]

Ann was captured. "Redeeming love . . . was now her theme," a friend remarked. "One might spend days with her without hearing any other subject reverted to."[3]

Perhaps it was that which caused Adoniram Judson, an aspiring young missionary, to notice Ann on the day of his commissioning. Scarcely a month later, Judson wrote a letter to his would-be father-in-law, asking whether he could "consent to part with [his] daughter early next spring, to see her no more in this world."[4] Adoniram had counted the cost of his mission and itemized its risks. And Ann was ready to do the same. With her parents' blessing she penned this response:

> O, if [Christ] will condescend to make me useful in promoting his kingdom, I care not where I perform his work, nor how hard it be. Behold the handmaid of the Lord; be it unto me according to thy word.[5]

## THE MARRIAGE, THE MISSION

Adoniram and Ann were married on February 5, 1812. That same day a farewell service was held for them and fellow missionaries Samuel and Harriet Newell. On February 22, en route to Burma, Ann wrote:

*O for a heart to live near to God, and serve him faithfully. . . . I should feel happy in the consideration of having left my native land, and my father's house, if by making this sacrifice, the kingdom of Christ would be promoted. May it be my great object to live a useful, holy life, and prepare to die a peaceful death.*[6]

Ann spent the remainder of her years doing just that. In just fourteen years she spent it all:

- Teaching and sharing the gospel, resulting in several female converts as well as translation work in Burmese and Siamese

- When her husband was imprisoned for his work, lobbying tirelessly for his release and improvement of his conditions, walking miles every day in scorching heat to deliver food and comfort measures to him and other prisoners

- Writing *An Account of the American Baptist Mission to the Burman Empire*, which was widely circulated in the United States and Britain, creating enormous interest in and funding for overseas missions

- Advancing and advocating for the education of women, teaching literacy and starting schools everywhere she traveled

All this she accomplished while enduring constant illness, the heart-wrenching loss of two of her three children, and long periods of separation from her beloved "Mr. J." In one of her last letters she wrote, "Oh! How much we owe to that kind Being who has mingled mercy with all our afflictions."[7] She had indeed counted the cost and was ready to pay the price—for Christ, for her husband, for Burma.

And pay the price she did. Ann died on October 24, 1826, at the age of thirty-seven from spotted fever (now known as cerebrospinal meningitis). Adoniram endured a period of deep depression following Ann's death but continued to minister in Burma for another twenty-four years until his death. During that time, he married and buried two more wives, Sarah and Emily, each of whom had been inspired to pursue missions as a result of Ann's writings.

## THE TRAIL SHE BLAZED

Ann Judson ran with fearless abandon toward whatever God had for her. "Not a hair of our head can be injured," she penned, "but with the permission of Him whose precious name we would make known."[8]

Ann's heart was that the women of Burma would be educated—that they would read, write, think, and use their minds to apply biblical truth to their lives. She wrote in "Address to Females in America":

> Shall we sit down in indolence and ease, indulge in all the luxuries with which we are surrounded, and which our country so bountifully affords, and leave beings like these, flesh and blood, intellect and feeling, like ourselves, and of our own sex, to perish, to sink into eternal misery? No! By all the tender feelings of which the female mind is susceptible, by all the privileges and blessings resulting from the cultivation and expansion of the human mind, by our duty to God and our fellow creatures, and by the blood and groans of Him who died on Calvary, let us make a united effort, let us call on all, old and young in the circle of our acquaintance, to join us in attempting to meliorate the situation, to instruct, to enlighten, and save females in the Eastern world; and though time and circumstances should prove that our united exertions have been ineffectual, we shall escape at death that bitter thought, that Burman females have been lost, without an effort of ours to prevent their ruin.[9]

Many of us live in communities chock-full of educated women, yet so many, even within our churches, are biblically illiterate. May we work out our mission to these women with a fervor that honors this great heroine of the faith and her Lord.

### About Laura

Born and raised in Michigan's Upper Peninsula, Laura Elliott and her husband, Michael, now call Minnesota home. In addition to being a mother of six, Laura is a writer, editor, and the marketing content manager for *Revive Our Hearts*. A woman from Christian history whom Laura admires is poet and hymn writer Fanny Crosby, to whose epitaph she also aspires: "Aunt Fannie: She hath done what she could."

# Take It Home, Make It Personal

1. When reflecting on her teen years, Ann said that she was "rapidly verging toward eternal ruin," and that she was "wild and volatile." How would you describe your teenage years?

2. Ann believed, "Not a hair of our head can be injured but with the permission of Him whose precious name we would make known." How would applying this truth to your life impact the way you live?

3. Ann's desire was to see the women of Burma educated and applying the Bible to their lives. Name one woman who has helped teach you to think more deeply about God. Then name one woman you can help to better understand and live out God's Word.

_____

_____

_____

_____

_____

_____

_____

_____

_____

_____

_____

# Pandita Ramabai

## Scholar, Reformer, Truth Seeker

Samantha Loucks

## CHAPTER 6: PANDITA RAMABAI

Born in India to high-caste Brahmin parents in 1858, Pandita Ramabai grew up fully immersed in the Hindu religion.

Her father stood against religious protocol when he chose to teach his wife and children to read and write Sanskrit. Though leaders labeled him a heretic for this, his daughter began reading sacred Hindu religious writings at the age of eight. Her family earned a living by reading the Puranas (sacred Hindu texts) in prominent public places, where listeners—if they were truly religious—were expected to bestow gifts such as flowers, garments, money, and food.

The Hindu religion was all Pandita and her family knew; they believed it was entirely sufficient for life and culturally proper according to their high caste. "We were not fit to do any other work to earn our livelihood, as we had grown up in perfect ignorance of anything outside the sacred literature of the Hindus," Pandita later wrote. "Our parents had unbounded faith in what the sacred books said. They encouraged us to look to the gods to get our support."[1]

But soon a famine left her family unable to earn anything through the religious works they so depended on. "At last, all the money which we had was spent, but the gods did not help us," she wrote. "We suffered from famine which we had brought upon ourselves."[2] Pandita's father, mother, and sister died from starvation, leaving Pandita and her brother utterly destitute.

She and her brother became wanderers, traveling more than four thousand miles on foot, bathing in rivers, and surviving on what scraps they were able to find. They continued to hope in the gods of their deeply rooted religious heritage, but time and again they were left disillusioned and dissatisfied. "We had fulfilled all the conditions laid down in the sacred books, and kept all the rules as far as our knowledge went, but the gods were not pleased with us and did not appear to us."[3]

Eventually Pandita's hope in Hindu gods began to grow cold. As her feet wandered through India, her defeated heart began to wander in pursuit of truth.

## SEARCHING FOR SOMETHING THAT WOULD SATISFY

In 1878, Pandita and her brother arrived in Calcutta (now officially Kolkata), where she encountered other religions, becoming even more confused and skeptical in the process. She first encountered Christianity at a gathering she attended by invitation. The Christians she met were kind to her, and a missionary gave her a Bible in Sanskrit. She thought the book was beautiful, but the teachings were strange and almost off-putting, certainly different from anything she'd ever heard.

Driven both by scholarly inclination and a thirst for teachings that would satisfy her, Pandita went on to study a wide range of religious writings. As a well-read woman, she found work in Calcutta lecturing women on their duties according to Hindu law. But the deeper she went in her studies, the more she experienced frustration and grave hopelessness for the women she was addressing.

According to Hindu teachings, a woman's only path for achieving liberation was through total abandonment to her husband. As Pandita summed it up, "She is to worship him with wholehearted devotion as the only god, to know and see no other pleasure in life except in the most degraded slavery to him."[4] Pandita found herself deeply bothered by this, and God continued to draw her toward Himself through her discomfort:

> My eyes were being gradually opened; I was waking up to my own hopeless condition as a woman, and it was becoming clearer and clearer to me that I had no place anywhere as far as religious consolation was concerned. I became quite dissatisfied with myself. I wanted something more than [this religion] could give me, but I did not know what it was that I wanted.[5]

All the detailed religious practices and worship Pandita grew up with had proven futile. The Hindu gods hadn't come through when she most needed help. Her religious studies were proving unsatisfactory, and as a woman she saw little hope for blessing in her future. So she kept searching.

## ENCOUNTERING LOVE

At age twenty-two Pandita married a Bengali man of lower caste and had a baby girl, but her husband died of cholera within the first two years of their marriage. Shortly afterward, through her studies, she became connected with Christians and Christian missionaries. She developed an interest in learning English and enjoyed the Christians' help and teaching.

In 1883 Pandita traveled to England to study and lived with nuns who invested in her life. She observed the women's rescue work and could hardly believe the mercy and compassion that was shown to sick, weak, and destitute women. In India these poor people would have been outcasts. No one would care to even look upon them. But through this mission's work, Pandita began to taste and see the goodness of God's love for all people.

Eager to know more, she asked the sisters to explain their motivation for such compassion. She read about Jesus' encounter with the Samaritan woman at the well in John 4.

> I had never read or heard anything like this in the religious books of the Hindus; I realized, after reading the fourth chapter of St. John's Gospel, that Christ was truly the Divine Saviour He claimed to be, and no one but He could transform and uplift the downtrodden womanhood of India and of every land. Thus my heart was drawn to the religion of Christ.[6]

But Pandita had merely found a religion that satisfied her intellectually; she hadn't yet truly encountered Christ in saving faith. It took eight more years before she truly recognized her sin and found her Savior in Jesus Christ.

## FOR GOD SO LOVED THE WORLD—THE WHOLE WORLD

Pandita's heart was radically changed, and so was her worldview. She came to believe the gospel is meant for everyone, available to anyone—a concept foreign to her hierarchical Indian culture. This transformational heart change would lead her to break chains in the caste-system culture as she provided assistance to the abandoned and despised.

Pandita had been wishing that someone would engage in ministry to help poor and destitute women in India, and God impressed upon her heart that it was her calling. In 1889 she founded Ramabai Mukti Mission—a ministry that still exists today—to provide assistance and hope to poor, abandoned, and abused Indian women and orphaned children.

Mukti Mission serves women and children by providing food, clothing, housing, and education, regardless of caste. The ministry's mission statement is beautifully gospel-centered: "Christ-centered homes where destitute women and children irrespective of their background—are accepted, cared for, transformed and empowered to be Salt & Light in the society."[7]

May we all have Pandita Ramabai hearts—hearts so captured by the saving power of Christ that we can't help but sing of His goodness. Hearts that see our spheres of influence as our mission fields. Hearts that love others unconditionally, no matter their rank or position.

## About Samantha

Samantha Loucks loves lazy lake days, strong coffee, and writing about the ways Jesus transforms our everyday messes into beautiful stories. She digs the four seasons in northern Indiana, is probably wearing a Notre Dame crewneck, and serves as the social-media manager on the *Revive Our Hearts* staff. Samantha admires Sabina Wurmbrand's radical commitment to serving oppressed people, despite imprisonment and immense suffering, because the gospel that sets us free is not threatened by wordly oppression or bound by prison walls!

# Take It Home, Make It Personal

1. As Pandita studied Hindu law, she found the practices futile and hopeless. Through her dissatisfaction God drew her to Himself. What are some ways that God has used dissatisfaction in your life to show you that He is the only One who can truly satisfy your soul?

2. Describe the sphere of influence that God has given you. What would it look like for you to treat the place where you are in as your mission field?

3. Pandita began to taste and see the goodness of God's love after reading about Jesus' encounter with the Samaritan woman at the well. Read John 4, asking God to draw your heart to the Savior who is able to transform and uplift downtrodden women.

_____

_____

_____

_____

_____

_____

_____

_____

_____

_____

_____

_____

CHAPTER 7

*Susanna Wesley*

A Hero Without a Cape

Erin Davis

## CHAPTER 7: SUSANNA WESLEY

I want to be a hero. I want to save the day, stop the villain, and rescue those in peril. But most days I can barely find my sneakers, much less a hero's cape. I just don't have the strength or the energy to leap buildings in a single bound. More often than not, the cares of life make me the one who needs to be rescued instead of the one swooping in to save others. That doesn't mean I have to let go of my dreams. As it turns out, cape owning and building leaping are not hero requirements.

### A DIFFERENT KIND OF HERO

Studying Christian history is a worthy pursuit because it reminds us of the superheroes of our faith. Consider the Wesley brothers, John and Charles.

John was an eighteenth-century English preacher and theologian credited with the revival that eventually became the Methodist church. John's brother, Charles, also played a key role in the Methodist revival. You may not know much about Charles, but I'm sure you've sung hymns he wrote, including "Christ the Lord Is Risen Today" and "Hark! The Herald Angels Sing."

John and Charles Wesley's efforts impacted millions of lives for Jesus. But where did their love for Christ and passion to see His Word preached come from?

*Enter the undercover hero of this story—their momma.*

She may not have worn a cape, but the Wesley brothers' mom, Susanna Wesley, is certainly a hero. She gave birth to nineteen children in twenty-one years. Only ten of those babies survived beyond the age of two. But through it all, Susanna depended on Christ with a contagious ferocity. She educated her children, launched a home church while her preaching husband was away, and took responsibility for her children's souls.

## A DIFFERENT KIND OF CAPE

Because of the gospel's impact on her own life, Susanna knew better than to try to disciple her large brood in her own strength. When she needed time alone, Susanna sometimes pulled her apron up over her head—a clear cue to her children to leave their mom alone. Susanna wasn't hiding under her smock for "me time" but to pray for herself and her family. Those prayers bore fruit in her children's lives and multiplied to reach millions.

I don't often wear an apron, but Susanna's story reminds me of some critical truths for mothering my own growing boys. Truths like:

- Prayer is my primary work.

- Get time with the Lord at all costs, even if you have to duck and cover in the kitchen.

- Watching me passionately serve Christ plants the seed of service in my children's hearts.

- Motherhood is hard but worth it.

We can all glean something from Susanna's approach. We find a blueprint for how this hero lived out her faith in some of the rules of her household:

- Subdue self-will in a child, and thus work together with God to save the child's soul.

- Teach a child to pray as soon as he can speak.

- Require all to be still during family worship.

- To prevent lying, punish no fault which is first confessed and repented of.

- Never allow a sinful act to go unpunished.

- Teach children to fear the rod.

- Never punish a child twice for a single offense.

- Commend and reward good behavior.

- Any attempt to please, even if poorly performed, should be commended.

- Strictly observe all promises.[1]

Any woman who takes training her children so seriously is a hero in my book. Her sons may have made some important gains for the kingdom, but their momma led them to their secret source of strength.

## STANDING ON SUSANNA'S SHOULDERS

I once heard it said that if the AIDS problem in Africa is going to be solved, mothers will solve it. I believe that's true. Moms have what politicians, doctors, and relief organizations lack—a momma-bear instinct to do whatever is necessary to protect our children. And moms like Susanna who apply that God-given tenacity to discipling their children might as well strap on a bright red cape. Christian moms (and dads) can be the superheroes God uses to fight the evil that tries to rise against our families.

We won't all parent exactly the way Susanna did. (There's no way I can get all of my children to be still during worship!) But we can stand on her shoulders by agreeing with her that motherhood is a high and holy calling and seeing our own homes as the place where we can be heroes by pointing our children to Christ.

## SENDING OUT THE BAT-SIGNAL

Batman probably ranks high on most lists of superheroes. Who doesn't admire his leather pantsuit and underground lair? But my favorite Batman accessory is the bat-signal. When Gotham City is in trouble, they shine a giant searchlight with a stylized bat shape on it, and their hero swoops down to save the day.

I join Susanna in sending out the bat-signal to you, moms. Our culture is in danger of losing sight of the family's value and the critical role only mothers can play. Our children are in danger of shouldering our anger, frustration, and bitterness if we can't choose to see them as God-given blessings. And we are in danger of missing an important mission the Lord has for us—to mother.

God has sent out the bat-signal to parents for generations. If we look in His Word, we find countless calls to make teaching and living our faith out at home a high priority. When we look back through the pages of history, we see mommas like Susanna who didn't do it perfectly but made a difference by mothering with kingdom priorities.

Let us hide under our aprons and strap on our capes. Let's rise to God's calling to swim upstream by asking Him to shift our focus beyond the trivial tasks of motherhood and toward using every moment to point others to Him.

## About Erin

Erin Davis is a writer and teacher passionately committed to getting women of all ages to the deep well of God's Word. She is the author of more than a dozen books and Bible studies, including *Connected*, *Beyond Bath Time*, and *7 Feasts*. Erin serves as content manager for *Revive Our Hearts* and hosts the *Women of the Bible* podcast and *Grounded* videocast. You can hear her teach on *The Deep Well with Erin Davis* podcast. The woman Erin admires most from Christian history is Helen Rosevere because she suffered and served with her eyes ever focused on Jesus.

# Take It Home, Make It Personal

1. How do you define a hero? Would Susanna Wesley meet those requirements?

2. Do you agree with Susanna that motherhood is a high and holy calling? Why do you think that families matter to society?

3. Read 1 Timothy 5:10, asking God to shift your focus from beyond the trivial tasks of everyday life toward using every moment to point others to Him.

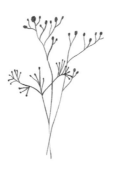

*"I always told God, I'm going to hold steady*
*on you, an' you've got to see me through."*

CHAPTER 8

# Harriet Tubman
## A Passion for Freedom

Mindy Kroesche

## CHAPTER 8: HARRIET TUBMAN

Harriet Tubman was born into slavery around 1820 in Maryland. Araminta Ross, or "Minty," as her family called her, began working as a slave at just five years old, when she was hired out to a neighbor. During the day she had a full load of domestic tasks and cared for a baby. At night she was to keep the baby from disturbing the master and mistress. When the little one cried out, the mother got up to whip Araminta. If she didn't do well enough at her household tasks, she was punished. In later years she remembered a day when she was whipped five times before breakfast.

One day when she was a teenager, Araminta tried to block the way of an angry overseer who was pursuing another slave. The overseer picked up a two-pound weight and threw it at the other slave—hitting Araminta in the head instead. Although she recovered, for the rest of her life she suffered from seizures that caused her to fall asleep without notice.

### ESCAPE TO FREEDOM

When she was just nineteen, Araminta married John Tubman, a free Black man. At this time she changed her name to Harriet to honor her mother. Although John was free, Harriet was still a slave—as would be any children they bore. After five years of marriage there were no children, and Harriet longed to flee to the North and freedom, but her husband did not share that desire.

Harriet had a deep faith in God. Although she was illiterate, her mother had taught her Bible stories and verses, laying a lasting spiritual foundation. Harriet began to pray for her master to become a Christian so he would set her and her family free. But when she heard a rumor that he was going to sell her, her prayers changed: "Lord, if you ain't never going to change that man's heart, *kill him*, Lord, and take him out of the way so he won't do any more mischief."[1]

Not long after that her master died, and Harriet felt intense guilt. But she also experienced a turning point: she vowed to escape!

In the fall of 1849, Harriet headed north, utilizing the resources of the Underground Railroad (UGRR), a loosely organized system of people aiding slaves to escape. While her husband refused to accompany her, two of her brothers joined her for a while before turning back. Harriet kept on. She moved at night and rested during the day, making most of her ninety-mile journey on foot. She settled in Philadelphia, which had a large community of free Black people. But although she had found freedom, she missed her family. After one year she faced another turning point that would make her famous.

## LIFE AS A CONDUCTOR

Harriet's family sent her a message that her niece was about to be sold into the deep South along with her niece's two little girls. Harriet felt a tug between her own freedom and her desire to help her family experience freedom too. She felt impressed by God: "It's you I want, Harriet Tubman."[2] From that point on she relied on her heavenly Father for wisdom, guidance, and strength. "I always told God," she said, "I'm going to hold steady on you, an' you've got to see me through."[3]

Harriet risked her life and safety as she traveled repeatedly back into Maryland to guide her family and other slaves to freedom. When she went back for her husband, she discovered he had taken another wife. Although deeply hurt, she focused on helping other fugitive slaves escape, taking many of them all the way to Canada.

Harriet became one of the most famous "conductors" of the UGRR and was nicknamed "Moses" for leading her people to freedom. Starting in 1852, Harriet made at least one trip a year into slave territory, helping at least ten fugitives at a time escape. Although her actions put a price on her head, she and those she helped were never captured. Many years after the Civil War had ended, Harriet boasted, "I was conductor of the Underground Railroad for eight years, and I can say what most conductors can't say—I never ran my train off the track and I never lost a passenger."[4]

Harriet was fearless. Thomas Garrett, an abolitionist and leader of the UGRR, said to a friend, "Harriet seems to have a special angel to guard her on her journey of mercy . . . and confidence [that] God will preserve her from harm."[5]

Harriet did have many close calls with patrols looking for runaway slaves, people she had known as a slave, even former masters. But she trusted God and asked Him to direct her—which, she said, "He always did."[6]

Exactly how many people Harriet rescued is unknown, but the number is estimated in the hundreds. She also often spoke at abolitionist meetings, captivating audiences both White and Black.

## A NEW ROLE

With the outbreak of the Civil War, Harriet took on a new role in her fight for freedom, working as a laundress, nurse, and armed scout and spy for the Union Army. She also helped freed slaves adjust to their new lives, often using her own limited funds.

When the war ended, Harriet settled in Auburn, New York, and devoted herself to helping others. Her good friend William H. Seward (a senator and former secretary of state) sold her a plot of land, where she created a home for her family and others in need. She campaigned for the women's suffrage movement and sought donations for orphans, the elderly, and disabled veterans.

One of the people Harriet took into her household was Nelson Davis, a war veteran and former slave who suffered from tuberculosis. Around this time Harriet learned that John Tubman had been killed in a violent argument with another man. Now a widow, she believed she was free to remarry. On March 18, 1869, Harriet and Nelson Davis married. Nelson was only twenty-five years old, and Harriet was at least twenty years his senior. They were happily married for almost twenty years.

In 1903 Harriet donated some of her land to the African Methodist Episcopal Church in Auburn. On this site the Harriet Tubman Home for the Aged opened in 1908. Eventually, when her health declined, Harriet herself entered the facility. On March 10, 1913, she died of pneumonia, surrounded by family and friends.

Not content to enjoy freedom for only herself, Harriet Tubman worked tirelessly to help others escape their own bondage. Even after the end of slavery, she continued to work for the benefit of others until she could do so no longer. Are we just as passionate about helping others escape bondage and find freedom in Christ?

## About Mindy

Mindy Kroesche lives on a small acreage in the Midwest with her husband and two kids. She likes relaxing at the lake with her family, curling up with a cozy mystery, and finding out what coffee shops serve the best raspberry mochas. Mindy is inspired by the stories of women like Elisabeth Elliot, Gladys Aylward, and Corrie ten Boom who chose to trust and obey the Lord no matter what.

# Take It Home, Make It Personal

1. Harriet relied on her heavenly Father, telling Him, "I'm going to hold steady on you, an' you've got to see me through." How have you seen God hold you during hard seasons?

2. In the midst of close calls, Harriet trusted God and asked Him to direct her, which, she said, "He always did." In what areas of your life are you looking to God for guidance?

3. Harriet was not content to enjoy freedom for herself; she also worked tirelessly to help others. Are you passionate about helping others escape bondage and find freedom in Christ?

*"The needs of these people*
*press upon my soul,*
*and I cannot be silent."*

# Lottie Moon
## A Story of Lifelong Sacrifice

Sheila Gosney

## CHAPTER 9: LOTTIE MOON

God's ways are higher than our ways, and sometimes God's plans are anything but typical. Such was the life of Lottie Moon, revered by many for a lifetime of service to Christ and for pioneering a missions movement that goes on to this day.

Charlotte Diggs "Lottie" Moon was born December 12, 1840, in Virginia to a well-to-do, strongly Christian family. Lottie attended Albemarle Female Institute in Virginia and went on to Hollins University, graduating in 1861. While in college Lottie achieved the highest grades of anyone in her class. She was one of the first Southern women to receive a master's degree.

### A LIFE-CHANGING DECISION

In 1858 Lottie gave her life to Christ after hearing the gospel at a series of revival meetings. Jesus was now her Savior, but she had no idea how much her life was going to change because of Him.

After college Lottie became a schoolteacher for girls in Danville, Kentucky. Later on she and a friend started a new school in Cartersville, Georgia. Lottie was recognized by those who met her as an intelligent and well-educated go-getter. Yet even as she was enjoying success in her chosen field, a yearning began to stir in her heart for something different and bigger than all her plans.

### A SISTER'S IMPACT

In 1872 Lottie's sister Edmonia ("Eddie") traveled to China as a missionary. Lottie was deeply touched by her sister's letters, which expressed how dire the spiritual need was in China and how desperate they were for more missionaries. While listening to a sermon on John 4:35, Lottie felt an undeniable conviction from God that China was her "white field" to harvest for Christ.

In 1873, at the age of thirty-two, Lottie sailed for China, leaving behind her family and her beloved school as well as a broken engagement. She had ended the relationship due to differing beliefs she and her fiancée held regarding the authority of the Bible and the call to serve Christ wholeheartedly on the mission field.

## WINNING THE CHINESE WITH LOVE

After arriving in China, Lottie taught school there for thirteen years. During that time she learned what the apostle Paul meant in 1 Corinthians 9:20 when he "became as a Jew" in order to win Jews. To connect with the Chinese people she met, she learned their language and studied the country's history. She even adopted Chinese dress. Even though she encountered suspicions and prejudice, this didn't discourage her. She simply grew more determined to love the Chinese people and introduce them to Jesus.

Lottie became a friend and helper to many in the villages where she taught, doing whatever she could to meet their physical and emotional needs. She was especially known for her ministry to the Chinese women. As she gained the trust of those she worked with, her popularity grew, and it wasn't uncommon for people to walk many miles to hear the teacher who "knew the Words of Life."

## CHANGING ROLES

In 1885, at age forty-five, Lottie gave up teaching and became a full-time missionary in the cities of P'ingtu and Tungchow (now Pingdu and Penglai). She would establish a new church; then an ordained minister would begin preaching and the gospel would spread. More than a thousand souls came to Christ.

While serving in P'ingtu, Lottie noticed how shy the Chinese children were around her. She started baking cookies to build relationships with them. Of course the children loved these treats! As her connection with the children grew, Lottie met their mothers and shared Christ with them.

Lottie persevered through much suffering for decades to advance the cause of Christ: the plague, smallpox, and the threat of persecution. Born into a life of financial blessing, Lottie learned to graciously make do on very little.

## A MASTER OF CORRESPONDENCE

While serving in China, Lottie wrote many letters back to the United States to her fellow Southern Baptists. Lottie's letters were firm in expressing that they were not doing enough for the sake of missions. Her charge was always more sacrifice, more prayer, and the need for more missionaries.

Lottie's passion for Christ shone in her many letters:

> *The needs of these people press upon my soul, and I cannot be silent. It is grievous to think of these human souls going down to death without even one opportunity of hearing the name of Jesus. (November 11, 1878, P'ingtu)*[1]

> *Why should we not . . . instead of the paltry offerings we make, do something that will prove that we are really in earnest in claiming to be followers of him who, though he was rich, for our sake became poor? (September 15, 1887, Tungchow)*[2]

Because of Lottie's eloquent pleas, a special offering was taken in 1881 by her childhood church. By 1888 Southern Baptist women had collected $3,315 to send more missionaries to China. In 1918 the WMU (Woman's Missionary Union) named their annual Christmas offering after Lottie Moon. This offering continues today and provides half of the Southern Baptist Convention's International Mission Board budget.

## END OF A MINISTRY, BEGINNING OF A LEGACY

Lottie Moon served selflessly and considered the needs of the Chinese people as greater than her own. She made great sacrifices for the sake of those who were suffering, readily giving her own food away and once sending her entire savings to her Chinese friends in P'ingtu who were suffering from famine.

In 1912, a very frail Lottie, suffering from an acute health problem, was ordered by her doctor to head back to the United States for rest and medical care. Four days into the journey, she died on the ship.

Lottie Moon truly gave her all to Christ and to the people of China. Many years prior to her death, she said, "I would that I had a thousand lives that I might give them to the women of China."[3] Lottie's story is a vivid reminder that God can use anything, even something as small as a cookie, to show love and build relationships for the sake of the gospel.

## About Sheila

Sheila Gosney lives in Missouri and is blessed with a husband, three sons, one daughter-in-law, two grandsons, and an incredible circle of family and friends. In her local church she enjoys teaching kids, mentoring younger women, and ministering with food. Sheila admires many women of God, but one she admires the most from Christian history is Lottie Moon and her entire life story of sacrifice for the sake of the gospel. Lottie truly lived for Christ in every way, and countless souls were won to Him through the years she demonstrated His love to the Chinese people.

# Take It Home, Make It Personal

1. When Lottie gave her life to Christ, she had no idea how much her life was going to change because of Him. How has trusting Jesus as your Savior changed your life?

2. As a missionary Lottie baked cookies to build relationships with nearby children and their mothers. What small acts of kindness could you engage in this week to help build relationships with those around you?

3. Read 2 Corinthians 8:8–10 and summarize what it says.

_____

_____

_____

_____

_____

_____

_____

*"'Twas mercy brought me
from my Pagan land
Taught my benighted soul to understand
That there's a God,
that there's a Saviour too."*

# *Phillis Wheatley Peters*
## Groundbreaking Poet with a Purpose

### Karen Ellis

# CHAPTER 10: PHILLIS WHEATLEY PETERS

The indomitable strength and grace of early-American poet Phillis Wheatley were first forged when she was kidnapped as a child from her home in Senegambia, West Africa, and forced into slavery. After enduring the horrific Middle Passage sea journey to North America, Phillis was purchased at auction by the Wheatley household. Her owners, John and Susanna Wheatley, were wealthy Bostonians who displayed their wealth through Phillis' presence. She was considered their luxury appendage: their "one slave owned for life." To own such a slave was, at the time, a status symbol indulged in by only one hundred nineteen slave owners in Boston.

In a twist of brutal irony, the young girl (probably about seven or eight) was given the name of the slaving vessel that had brought her to America—the *Phillis*. Because she had been stolen from the region of Africa where the slavers felt "domestic help" was best "cultivated," the intent was to train her as a domestic servant. The Wheatleys' daughter, Mary, was tasked with teaching Phillis the English language so she could navigate her servant role, and their son, John, later helped teach her as well. Yet the student soon surpassed both teachers in their rudimentary lessons. And as Phillis began to hunger after the Christian faith, her religious and theological education was taken over by the Reverend George Sewall at the Old South Congregational Church in Boston.

It is understandable that possible manumission made Christianity attractive to many slaves. Yet Phillis' conversion seems to have been profound and genuine, and wonder and gratitude mark her later religious works. Her "Hymn to Humanity" proclaims, for example:

> Lo! For this dark terrestrial ball
> Forsakes his azure-paved hall
>     A prince of Heav'nly birth!
> Divine Humanity behold.
> What wonders rise, what charms unfold
> At his descent to earth![1]

It was God's providence that gave Phillis an education of such depth in a world that doubted her humanity and intellectual ability.

By age nine Phillis was reading English with fluency and ease from the most difficult portions of the Bible. No doubt what seemed an intellectual impossibility to those around her provided dignity, identity, and comfort as she pressed into her God-given purpose. In addition to reading sacred texts in English, at ten years old she mastered Greek and Latin, reading the classic works of writers like Ovid and even translating Virgil into English. By age fourteen she was fully catechized in her church and also published for the first time. At sixteen she became an official member of the Old South Congregational Church.

## GENIUS CHILD, GENIUS WORK

As her brilliance shone through trauma and fear, Phillis confounded the narrow categories into which she had been confined. In 1773 Susanna Wheatley helped finance the publishing of Phillis' first literary work. *Poems on Various Subjects, Religious and Moral* was issued as a small octavo edition in England and quickly gained popularity. This work became a landmark achievement in American history, making Phillis the first African American woman to publish a book of poems.

As Phillis grew into womanhood, her artistic reputation grew also. She produced literary works in two styles: a provincial style that dealt with the local and global issues of the day and a classical style that echoed works by Ovid, Virgil, and Homer.

It is clear that Phillis loved language and Scripture. Her reflections on God are undergirded by themes of redemption, biblical authority, God's image and providence, original sin, depravity, righteous suffering, the coming kingdom, and humanity's need of the Savior. With access to both her English Bibles and the original languages, she came to understand that chattel slavery and African inferiority were not only inconsistent with the teachings of Christ through the Gospels but also with those of Old Testament Israel. She expresses this conviction in several of her works, which use Scripture to demonstrate that Africans and Europeans share a common humanity. Consider these lines from "On Being Brought from Africa to America," in which she seemingly revisits her Middle Passage experience but may actually also be alluding to the pagan land of unbelief and to the land of redemption and salvation in Christ, of which *all* humankind has need:

'Twas mercy brought me from my *Pagan* land
Taught my benighted soul to understand
That there's a God, that there's a *Saviour* too.
Once I redemption neither sought nor knew.
Some view our sable race with scornful eye;
"Their colour is a diabolic dye."
Remember, *Christians*, *Negroes*, black as *Cain*,
May be refin'd, and join th' angelic train.[2]

It was common to speak derisively of Africa as "the Dark Continent." But is Phillis here writing about the dark land of the African slave, or is she communicating in code about the dark land of the human soul? A careful reading suggests a hidden message for those both spiritually and physically enslaved. Literary analyst William J. Schieck asks us to look to these two lines for clues: "Remember, *Christians*, *Negros*, black as *Cain* / May be refin'd, and join th' angelic train."

If we read casually, we might think that Phillis is supporting the common pro-slavery teaching that the Black race is descended from Cain and is therefore marked as cursed with dark skin. However, a closer look reveals she does not name her "Pagan land," and it is capitalized. What could she be trying to tell us? Phillis certainly would have read about many Africans in Scripture, from Moses' wife to the Ethiopian eunuch. This locates God in her native Africa, dignifying Africans, long before the slavers arrived. William Schieck sheds new light on this literary device, pointing out the "indicative use of italicization for *Christians*, *Negros*, and *Cain*," and the subtle placement of the punctuation after the word "Negros." Though grammatically correct, the italicization and comma lend an air of ambiguity that names both Christians and Negroes as descendants of Cain—the "presumed saved" and the "presumed unsaved," all of humanity—sinful and in need of redemption and divine grace.[3]

Phillis often found ways to defeat the common belief of the day that the Black race was sub-human. She subtly reminds that original sin and total depravity infect all of humanity, rendering all equal in the sight of God, a sentiment she echoes in her "Hymn to Humanity." O'Neale calls her destruction of the Cain myth a dual "detoxification," first of the understanding of ancient biblical curse, and then of the entire race-based slavery system.[4]

When read from this perspective, Phillis puts the Cain narrative squarely back into its proper theological context, one that is consistent from Genesis to Revelation. In doing so, she stands for accurate biblical interpretation, for the humanity of those bound in circumstance by the color of their skin and for those eternally bound above it by the blood of Christ.[5]

## A WONDROUS LIFE

Famous but still not free, Phillis joined a few other like-minded individuals to begin some of the first recorded Christian mission work from the shores of colonial America. In 1774 they published Christian tracts that funded mission work in Ghana and in the settlements of freed Africans in Sierra Leone. Their mission work began eight years earlier than George Lisle's in the Caribbean and seventy-nine years before Hudson Taylor departed from England to China. But this mission work would have to be continued by another faithful team in another age because the Revolutionary War would soon cut their efforts short.

For the enslaved in eighteenth-century America, there were a number of avenues to emancipation. Some saved up money to purchase their freedom. Some took advantage of the so-called Mansfield option, which offered a tenuous freedom to slaves who were taken into a free jurisdiction. Still others chose to escape. Each choice was fraught with risk and loss. Phillis chose purchase and negotiation, the method of emancipation that appeared to grant her the most freedom. July 26, 1773, marked the date of her manumission in what she later called her *annus mirabilis*, her wondrous year.

Yet the greater miracle was the transformation of the Wheatley family from pro-slavery to anti-slavery sentiment within just one generation. In light of the change in their hearts due to their relationship, Phillis chose to continue living with the next generation of Wheatleys after her emancipation. She supported herself, managed her own affairs, and came and went as a free woman.

Phillis Wheatley's last years were marked by difficulty. She married a grocer named John Peters and lost three children before dying herself at the age of thirty-one. Although her body lies in an unmarked and undiscovered grave, she lives in the presence of the Savior to whom she committed her life as a young girl. History may have lost Phillis Wheatley for a time, but her God did not. Her legacy as America's first African American poet continues to inspire those who wonder what a single person can accomplish in the face of massive challenges.

## About Karen

Karen Ellis is passionate about theology, human rights, and global religious freedom. She is the director of the Edmiston Center for the Study of the Bible and Ethnicity at Reformed Theological Seminary in Atlanta, where she is also a Robert Cannada fellow for world Christianity. Since 2006 she has collaborated with the Swiss-based organization International Christian Response and travels internationally advocating for marginalized, overlooked, persevering Christians—both in history and also the contemporary world.

# Take It Home, Make It Personal

1. How does Phillis' story display the gospel? Explain.

2. Read Phillis' poems again. What stirs you about them?

3. Consider your own story and legacy. What do you most hope people will say about you when you are gone?

_____

_____

_____

_____

_____

_____

_____

_____

# *Notes*

## Introduction

1. Amy Carmichael, *Candles in the Dark: Letters of Hope and Encouragement* (Fort Washington, PA: CLC, 1981), 31.

2. Charles Haddon Spurgeon, "The Spiritual Resurrection," sermon preached January 30, 1898, *Metropolitan Tabernacle Pulpit*, vol. 44, Spurgeon Center (Midwestern Baptist Theological Seminary), accessed March 4, 2022, www.spurgeon.org/resource-library/ sermons/the-spiritual-resurrection/#flipbook.

3. C. S. Lewis, *An Experiment in Criticism* (Cambridge, UK: Cambridge Univ. Press, 1961), 141.

## Mary Slessor

1. W. P. Livingstone, *Mary Slessor of Calabar: Pioneer Missionary*, 7th ed. (London: Hodder and Stoughton, 1916), 49, www.forgottenbooks. com/en/readbook/MarySlessorofCalabar_10196431#62.

2. Livingstone, 193.

3. Livingstone, 155.

4. Livingstone, 117.

5. A. Kennedy Curtis and Daniel Graves, *Great Women in Christian History: 37 Women Who Changed Their World*, (Pennsylvania: Christian Publications, Inc., 2004, 177.

6. Livingstone, 73–74.

### Sabina Wurmbrand

1. "Extreme Temptation (Repost)," *Persecution Blog*, Voice of the Martyrs, March 22, 2013, www.persecutionblog.com/2013/03/extreme-temptation-repost.html.

### Betty Scott Stam

1. Betty Scott Stam, 1925, quoted in Elisabeth Elliot, *Quest for Love* (Grand Rapids, MI: Revell, 1996), 131.

2. Stam, in Elliot, *Quest for Love*, 126–127.

3. Stam, quoted in "Stories of the Christian Martyrs: John and Betty Stam," *Stories*, Voices of the Martyrs (website), July 26, 2021, excerpted from John Foxe and Voices of the Martyrs, *Voices of the Martyrs: AD33–Today* (Washington, DC, Salem Books, 2019), www.persecution.com/stories/stories-of-christian-martyrs-john-and-betty-stam.

### Corrie ten Boom

1. Corrie ten Boom, John L. Sherrill, and Elizabeth Sherrill, *The Hiding Place*, 9th ed., (New York: Bantam, 1974), 45.

2. ten Boom, Sherrill, and Sherrill, 83.

3. ten Boom, Sherrill, and Sherrill, 107.

4. Corrie ten Boom and Jamie Buckingham, *Tramp for the Lord* (Fort Washington, PA: CLC, 1974), 15.

5. ten Boom, Sherrill, and Sherrill, 194.

6. ten Boom, Sherrill, and Sherrill, 238.

7. ten Boom, Sherrill, and Sherrill, 238.

## Ann Hasseltine Judson

1. Sharon James, "The Life and Significance of Ann Hasseltine Judson (1789–1826)," pdf download, *Journal of Missions*, SBJME 1/2 (fall 2012): 23, https://equip.sbts.edu/publications/journals/journal-of-missions/sbjme-12-fall/the-life-and-significance-of-ann-hasseltine-judson-1789-1826.

2. James, *My Heart in His Hands: Ann Judson of Burma, A Life, with Selections from her Memoir and Letters* (Darlington, UK: Evangelical Press, 1998), 24–26.

3. James, *Ann Judson: A Missionary Life for Burma, a Biography, including Selections from Her Memoir and Letters*, 7th ed. (Grand Rapids, MI: Evangelical Press, 2015), 29.

4. James, "Life and Significance of Ann Hasseltine Judson," 22.

5. Ann Hasseltine Judson and James Davis Knowles, *Memoir of Mrs. Ann H. Judson, Wife of the Rev. Adoniram Judson, Missionary to Burmah, with a History of the American Baptist Mission in the Burman Empire* (London: G. Wightman, 1838), 48.

6. Judson and Knowles, 55.

7. James, *Ann Judson: A Missionary Life for Burma*, 231.

8. James, *Ann Judson: A Missionary Life for Burma*, 172.

9. Judson and Knowles, 354.

## Pandita Ramabai

1. Pandita Ramabai, "The Pandita Ramabai Story in Her Own Words," pdf, Bible Teaching Program, March 1907, 3, accessed March 4, 2022, http://bibleteachingprogram.com/religion/panditaramabai.pdf.

2. Ramabai, 3.

3. Ramabai, 3–4.

4. Ramabai, 5.

5. Ramabai, 6.

6. Ramabai, 8.

7. "About the Mukti Mission," Pandita Ramabai Mukti Mission (website), accessed October 20, 2021, www.prmm.org.in/about-mukti-mission.

### Susanna Wesley

1. "Susanna Wesley's 16 Rules of Parenthood," The Mother's Heart (website), accessed March 9, 2022, http://www.openarmsmagazine.com/Susanna%20Wesley%20Rules.pdf.

### Harriet Tubman

1. Catherine Clinton, *Harriet Tubman: The Road to Freedom* (New York: Little Brown, 2004), 31.

2. Clinton, 83.

3. Mark Galli, "Harriet Tubman: Her Faith Fueled the Underground Railroad, *Today's Christian Woman*, November 1999, www.todayschristianwoman.com/articles/1999/november/harriet-tubman.html.

4. Clinton, 192.

5. Clinton, 91.

6. Ibid.

### Lottie Moon

1. Keith Harper, *Send the Light: Lottie Moon* (Macon: Mercer Univ. Press, 2002), 225.

2. Harper, 223.

3. Harper, 132.

## Phillis Wheatley

1. Phillis Wheatley, *Poems of Phillis Wheatley: A Native African and a Slave* (Bedford: Applewood, 1995), 61.

2. Wheatley, 12.

3. William J. Scheick, "Phillis Wheatley's Appropriation of Isaiah." *Early American Literature 27, no. 2* (1992), 136.

4. Sondra O'Neale, "A Slave's Subtle War: Phillis Wheatley's Use of Biblical Myth and Symbol." *Early American Literature 21, No. 2* (1986), 150–151.

5. O'Neale, "A Slave's Subtle War," 151–152. The Cain myth presumed that Africans were descendants of the son of Cain, and therefore were ontologically relegated to his stereotypical characteristics: animalistic and lustful behavior, the stain-mark of dark skin, a cursed relationship with the earth, displacement as a landless people, and eternal servitude to the elect (and presumably White) older brother. The "Curse of Cain" was often conflated with the "Curse of Ham."

# Authors

### Nancy DeMoss Wolgemuth

Nancy DeMoss Wolgemuth has touched the lives of
millions of women through two nationally syndicated radio
programs heard each day—*Revive Our Hearts* and *Seeking
Him*. Her books have sold more than five million copies.
Through her writing, podcasts, and events, Nancy is reaching
the hearts of women around the world, calling them to freedom,
fullness, and fruitfulness in Christ. Nancy is inspired by women like Selina
Hastings, Countess of Huntingdon (1707–1791), who used her considerable
resources and influence to help further the work of the first Great Awakening,
foreign missions, and the care of infants and children who had been abandoned
by their parents.

### Colleen Chao

Colleen Chao writes about God's goodness in her life
journey, which has included singleness, anxiety and
depression, chronic illness, and stage-four cancer. Colleen
makes her home near Boise, Idaho, with her husband, Eddie,
their son Jeremy, "the cat," and Willow the dog. The woman in Christian history
Colleen most admires is Amy Carmichael—for the way she loved Jesus and
cared for others out of her many sufferings.

### Erin Davis

Erin Davis is a writer and teacher passionately committed to
getting women of all ages to the deep well of God's Word.
She is the author of more than a dozen books and Bible
studies, including *Connected*, *Beyond Bath Time*, and

*7 Feasts*. Erin serves as content manager for *Revive Our Hearts* and hosts the *Women of the Bible* podcast and *Grounded* videocast. You can hear her teach on *The Deep Well with Erin Davis* podcast. The woman Erin admires most from Christian history is Helen Rosevere because she suffered and served with her eyes ever focused on Jesus.

## Hugh Duncan

Hugh Duncan serves as director of audio and video for *Revive Our Hearts*. He's married to Renae and is dad to Nora and Muriel. While working on audio projects about Billy Graham and Bill and Vonette Bright, he was struck by the influence of one woman from church history. Henrietta Mears, director of education at First Presbyterian Church of Hollywood, was a huge encouragement to a generation of leaders whose influence is still being felt today.

## Laura Elliott

Born and raised in Michigan's Upper Peninsula, Laura Elliott and her husband, Michael, now call Minnesota home. In addition to being a mother of six, Laura is a writer, editor, and the marketing content manager for *Revive Our Hearts*. A woman from Christian history whom Laura admires is poet and hymn writer Fanny Crosby, to whose epitaph she also aspires: "Aunt Fannie: She hath done what she could."

## Karen Ellis

Karen Ellis is passionate about theology, human rights, and global religious freedom. She is the director of the Edmiston Center for the Study of the Bible and Ethnicity at Reformed Theological Seminary in Atlanta, where she is also a Robert Cannada fellow for world Christianity. Since 2006 she has collaborated with the Swiss-based organization International Christian Response and travels internationally advocating for marginalized, overlooked, persevering Christians—both in history and also the contemporary world.

### Sheila Gosney

Sheila Gosney lives in Missouri and is blessed with a husband, three sons, one daughter-in-law, two grandsons, and an incredible circle of family and friends. In her local church she enjoys teaching kids, mentoring younger women, and ministering with food. Sheila admires many women of God, but one she admires the most from Christian  history is Lottie Moon and her entire life story of sacrifice for the sake of the gospel. Lottie truly lived for Christ in every way, and countless souls were won to Him through the years she demonstrated His love to the Chinese people.

### Mindy Kroesche

Mindy Kroesche lives on a small acreage in the Midwest with her husband and two kids. She likes relaxing at the lake with her family, curling up with a cozy mystery, and finding out what coffee shops serve the best raspberry mochas. Mindy is inspired by the stories of women like Elisabeth Elliot, Gladys Aylward, and Corrie ten Boom who chose to trust and obey the Lord no matter what.

### Samantha Loucks

Samantha Loucks loves lazy lake days, strong coffee, and writing about the ways Jesus transforms our everyday messes into beautiful stories. She digs the four seasons in northern Indiana, is probably wearing a Notre Dame crewneck, and serves as the social-media manager on the *Revive Our Hearts* staff. Samantha admires Sabina Wurmbrand's radical commitment to serving oppressed people, despite imprisonment and immense suffering, because the gospel that sets us free is not threatened by wordly oppression or bound by prison walls!

## Kelly Needham

Kelly Needham hopes to convince as many people as possible that nothing compares to knowing Jesus. She teaches the Bible at her home church where she coleads a women's teaching program, training women to accurately handle the word of truth. She is the author of *Friendish: Reclaiming Real Friendship in a Culture of Confusion* and is a frequent blogger and speaker. Kelly and her husband, Jimmy, have four children and live in the Dallas, Texas, area. Corrie ten Boom is one of Kelly's favorite women in Christian history because she exemplifies the power of daily, ordinary obedience to God.

## Jani Ortlund

Jani Ortlund, the vice president of Renewal Ministries, loves connecting women with the Word of God. Serving Christ through writing, speaking, and discipling is her chief passion in life. Jani, who podcasts at herestoresmysoul.org, and Ray, the president of Renewal Ministries, have four married children and fifteen grandchildren. One of the women from Christian history whom Jani greatly admires is Amy Carmichael. Jani is grateful for Amy's wholehearted devotion to Christ and her cheerful defiance as she pressed on no matter the cost to serve His purposes for her in her generation.

## Leanna Shepard

Leanna Shepard loves Jesus, mountains, blueberries, and spending time with family and friends. An ideal day for her starts with a hot cup of tea and ends with a good book. She is grateful for the women throughout history (both ancient and recent) who have pointed her to Jesus, including Hagar, Corrie ten Boom, and Elyse Fitzpatrick.

Calling Women to Freedom,
Fullness, and Fruitfulness in Christ

• Daily Teaching
• Resources
• Events
• Digital Media
• Broadcast Media

For more with Nancy DeMoss Wolgemuth, visit

**REVIVE** OUR **HEARTS** . COM

Your Trustworthy Source for Biblical Truth